A Collection of Verse

Nonfiction

Eliza Earsman

Please pay particular attention to the final poem:

'LEST SHE FORGETS.

Lest we.'

*****

*****

Dedication:

For justice—and decent people.

*****

Foreword

It is a pleasure to be in a position to encourage an interest in poetry. Too many of us didn't develop a love of fine literature and poetry because it was taught by teachers who had passion for story and words sapped from them when they, too, were young, and because they were forced to teach within the parameters of inept and colorless curriculums.

Part of the problem, of course, lies with poets themselves. It is easy to sing songs the same or similar to the ones we've heard before. I can't remember who said it recently--one of our US state's poet laureates, I think--that poets need to roam afar from the personal more often. Earsman does that, though the personal is always a subtext.

Earsman's passion is evident. She tackles both the familiar and the unexpected. She takes risks with recreations of dialect. She uses unfamiliar words, risks using the vernacular, favors what is authentic. She has been known to include glossaries with her work, a nod to the uninitiated, encouragement for those who would like to tackle poetry but don't care for the struggle.

Eliza, in other words, is a brave new poet with a future before her.

Carolyn Howard-Johnson

Multi award-winning poet and novelist

Instructor for the renowned University of California

(UCLA) Extension Writers' Program

Testimonials

"Those who are intrigued by political ingénue will find Eliza's Collection of Verse interesting reading."

—Lisa Lickel, USA.

"The poetry is emotional and vivid. Ms. Earsman splashes history throughout. This book is extremely thought provoking and edifying."

—Stacey Pierce, USA.

"Eliza instills a respect for nature in a non-preachy way that is neither simplistic nor obtuse."

—La Vaughn Kemnow, USA.

"Eliza Earsman's command of words, her experiential background, and her deep sense of perception are spellbinding in this book."

—Lorilyn Roberts, USA.

"A Collection of Verse most certainly, but an "Outstanding Collection of Verse" says it best."

—Salvatore Buttaci, USA.

"Peace and pleasure found here makes the book purchase so worth-while."

—Lori Finnila, USA.

"Eliza writes from the heart. Her words fly off the page and aim for your soul."

—Renee Wiggins, USA.

"Eliza's book deserves five stars for its daring, both politically and poetically."

—Carolyn Howard-Johnson, USA.

"Eliza's enthusiasm for Christianity, justice and history, shines through with every line, footnote and exclamation mark."

—Martha Engber, USA.

"A whisper of grace in each word gives breathe to a unique collection of poetry."

—Georgia Woodward, USA.

*****

About the Author

Christian author Eliza Earsman was born in the southern low-lands of Scotland.

As a member of international literary communities Eliza enjoys networking. She likes clean air and fresh people. Her travels include United States of America, Canada, Israel, Spain, Jordan, Portugal, Holland, Central and Eastern Europe, France, Australia, Scotland, Ireland, Malaysia and Korea.

In her autobiographical works (see below) Eliza does not always follow conventional methods, but brutally honest depictions in her published works have done much to raise international awareness about Freemasonry and Freemasonry's intended World War Three:

- Days of Elijah: A True Story—ISBN 978-0-9556248-2-7
- A Collection of Verse (Hardback)—ISBN 978-0-9556248-1-0
- Days of Elijah Film Script—ISBN 978-0-9556248-4-1

*****

Contents

NIGHT ON THE TILES
Peace Piping Screens:

The vessels started empty, change is taking space,
The mixture here is heady and air is being displaced
By the hugging–puffing–blowing,
The drag on air is blue,
Peace pipe's bubbles interacting
With the strong and rosy glow.
Afflicting lungs and rooms:
Fool dressed as flower-empowering weed.

The grass is always greener on the other side, they say,
Of the conscious mind's ability to select and shun the ways
Of intoxicating measure, liquid, leaves, converting power,
Contemplating life's new sure face, spinning, round,
Revolving doors.

Fewer rules requiring worry
Distance time and state and place,
Exhale of satisfaction—change is up and speed is pace.
Smug of distant fashion giving all a cheery glow
Coughing, spluttering, wheezing,
Drawing trouble, squeak and go.

Pipe dreams tubing interacting
With the smell, the smoke,
The seed.

And through the storm, smiles memories
Of tomorrow's distant haze
The area to be covered is only now 'til then.
Invest in speculating,
And clothed in now right mind
What suits us now is dear time
As we leave the world
Behind—the cares and sorrows—
To enjoy our journey on
The surface interceptors
Blocking daze and bright new dawn.

Psychedelic open highways,
Psychedelic open hues
Speeding brain cells along highways
That they've never been before.
Requisitioning soft *'ssshoo'* shuffling,
Nuclear shrinking as they're swelling,
As they're tossing and they're turning
Around corners seldom met—
Till they end up in collision
With the message that is set:

'Back off, back off, and calm down,
To base so freely given—

'Tis easy to reach there
In Scripture answer's given,
By the One who's watching over
The hearts and minds of all
Who in Creation's wonders, blunder,
And who wander off and fall.

To leaving interweaving
Shapes and colors, size and hue,
And to junk food store tobacco smoking out
Amazing Grace.

Through our lazy interaction the joker's ace is high;
Temptation's ready reckoning
Of the price there is to pay:
To juggle in the jungle of those so ill acquaint
With the niceties of nations—
Sparking out their discontent.

As the embers are washed out
And the ash is left behind
To be scuffed and kicked and trodden—
Returned unto the ground.

*****

The resolution surely of greater value then?
The hallelujah chorus is given free to each—new man.

HOME IN ON THE RANGE

Imagine a valley—fertile and green—
Cloud banks, thunder clears,
Rain debates then heads away.
'Neath that nectar making molten sky,
Day is breaking in.

Stands the high grasses,
'Dandy's down'* in the wind,
Air's stubborn fragrant sense,
Lilies' peace dells, and hanging bells.

Watered and growing—wander unseen—
By the blue-tops, the larch-laps,
The kookaburra swings.
Perri-winkles, popping poppers, ramble and see:
The range in the flower power—
And pollens' busy bees.

Bedded in treetops—
Squirrels pine, needles spruce.
Dense neighbor fern
Presents shade, shape and kind.
Tom thumbs, puff balls rise;
Roses ramble on.

Heather scent, the honey clover,
Wholesome and wild.

Little bug patrols. Earthworms mate.
Troops swarm—multi task and carry pouch—
Great big little bruisers turf and run.
Robust agile slender tiny sniffers listen, glean,
While having fun.

In barefoot synchronicity
Living throngs are sharing traits.
Sculpted overhang formations,
Grasses sway—worn overhead.

Through that rare view window—
Gruff old Billy's calling quits,
Shifts his necktie smartly,
Nibbles grass—then calmly sits.

From arrival to departure,
To the point of no return
Subtle seedlings' long translations
Broadcast strong amassing grace.

In fields of light fantastic,
Harvest's law of reap and sow
Navigates the transplantations,
Bloom—make love, and beauty, grow.

* Dandelion down.

SCHOOLDAYS

First day at school—my mother's hand—
'and off you go' says she.
'There's a rocking horse, it's big and high'
Uh hu. And she also told me
about the dentist's fish in the aquarium.
He had a drill and pliers.

'You'll like it fine, I'll collect you at three'.
So off I go tootling (1) in
Tae the 'Girls' on the richt,
And the 'Boys' tae the left
And the 'Jannie' (2) tae keep us in trim.

The building is braw (3) —all sandstone and stable
Built in the days when work was a pride,
And builders were skilled and that work that they left
Is still there at the top o' the town.

'Academy' meant that we all went together,
There wasn't another one there,
'Cept the fee paying ones dotted around,
But ours was the one 'yond compare.

The playground was great—it was smooth—
It was large, easy found.
Roller skates whizzed—and ball bearings
Went flying around.

The headmaster wasn't too keen on us dinners (4)
'Dinnae go quite so fast or I'll hae you put oot,
Keep it quiet, keep it neat, keep it doon'.

There werena' many bully boys—
We most were friends together.
The ones that were—what can be said?
Ah'll tell it then it's over:

His mither's (5) son was Johnny B,
And Peter Boyd as well.
Bleached brilliant white—aye, always clean
An very glakit (6) too,
'An dinnae play wi' such as they'—
Was drummed intae their skull.

The show was on—oh sic a sicht (7)
They didnae fool that many
They didnae ken (8),
Their mithers (9) didnae tell them,
The place to be on bended knee
Is the place before Our Father.

Ah didnae really want tae
Bring this tae the richt attention.
The teacher said a hud (10) tae
So ah'll gie the twa (11) a mention.

Johnny led a merry dance—
An noo he's fa'in (12) flat
His record shows the greasy pole—
He's makin' sure o' that.

Peter went to higher hichts (13)
A Chief Inspector's bunnet (14)
They ken him now—the silly male.
They come as ten a punnet.

Greasy fingers hae these boys
Ah ken, they're peddlin' mony (15)
But then, in global context,
They are but the few not many.

Their sins will find them oot, och aye—
The reason tells tae a'
Their mothers made them clean a richt
The OMO (16) did it a'.
The inside oot was never touched—
They didnae tell at all—
These twa (17) young boys were never telt (18)
It's inside oot (19).
That's a.

And now I'll have tae get on track
Away from that transgression.
Ah'll tell it as it really was—
Neils Haw can vouch this version.

Well many a laugh did we hae in that school,
And many a furrow an' a',
As we figured it quaint—
When Versailles (20) was pinned tae the wa'.
'And learn it by heart. Ye'll be tested on that'.

A monkey can dae that an' a.
'Dinnae ask questions, the history is old—
It's a' written down, don't ye see
The examiner wants the answer that's right,
So argue w' him no w' me'.

Maths was a richt (21)—a dinnae well see
Why algebra has tae be sic (22) a bore.
The teacher said 'Aye. Ah kin see whit ye mean'.
So 'oot' (23)—and he showed me the door.
Out in the fields, my mind was aye there—
But English was doing me well.
Her mission was fine and the teacher did a',
She telt (24) me o' much Up Abin (25).

'Just carry yer load and do it wi' pride,
Ah'll no be around ye tae see.
But we're a thinking well o' the times that are due (26).
And swear on The Bible—tell well.'

The 'Homecraft' was guid (27)
We sewed skirts with pride,
The mince and the tatties (28) tae stew.
We a' did our bit wi' the porridge and tripe
Miss Grigg's face was all of a glow.

A dinnae (29) often speak like this—
It's especially for the lesson.
We wur (30) brought up tae speak just right—
The Q's and P(lease)'s and Thank You's.
'Proper English'—and no bloody messing.

We did move on to the Secondary part
And a wis (31) their Gala Queen.
But times have moved on for many since that,
And I'm moving on and awa' (32).

And Canada* beckons frae (33) yon yonder parts
(*fa...ar* away—from Britain.)
And many can vouch that there's clean.
And looking back is a that this is
And I'm glad;
I'll not be back—
A gain.

[1] ambling
[2] janitor
[3] handsome/ well proportioned

⁴ noise makers
⁵ mother's
⁶ not too clever
⁷ such a sight
⁸ did not know
⁹ mothers
¹⁰ had
¹¹ two
¹² falling
¹³ heights
¹⁴ Police Chief Inspector's bonnet/hat
¹⁵ I know, they're peddling many (lives)/money
¹⁶ trade name for laundry powder.
¹⁷ two
¹⁸ told
¹⁹ out
²⁰ Treaty of Versailles
²¹ alright
²² such
²³ out
²⁴ told
²⁵ Up Above
²⁶ 40 years old—1987
²⁷ good
²⁸ potatoes
²⁹ I don't
³⁰ were
³¹ was
³² away
³³ from

BARRY
The Making of a Man.

He's a hard nut is Barry, just 13 years and old, so very old.
His mother's lover threw him out—
With baggage, stock and barrel.
The criminal police
Were at the respectable door—
And his mother didn't like it.

Toughening by the minute—but butter wouldn't melt—
In chain gang interaction he is finding easy meat.
In psychopath potential he's growing more and more
With knife he'll give a Glesga (1) grin—
And wouldnae (2) think a thing.

Not too bright is Barry on hormonal overload
Testosterone is swirling round—
'White Lighting' (3) adding to it.
They tend to gie (4) him money
To ferment his overload;
They dinnae (5) seem to gie a thought—
He's really needing more—
And folks around are paying,
Wi' their eyes and teeth and scars.

Ah seen him dae away (6) one night—
The bloke was on the ground.
The crowd around him was berserk,
And Barry to the fore.

A tin of beans (7) was in his hands—
The head one took a beating.
'Oh fellows, dinnae dae (8) that,
It's the stage o' dereliction.'

'Hullo Rose' little Barry says—
Potential manifesting.
Some day he's going to be a man—
He knows it and he told me.
He's working hard on details
That would take some disbelieving.

I don't know where he's going to go,
The options aren't many.
Maybe someday he'll lock that door
And walk in much—tae many.

I hae a word wi' God on High
To keep an eye on Barry.
Someday he'll maybe settle down
Wi' some nice tae marry.

An' break the vicious cycle
O' so many in transition.
Oh Holy Lord please make him see
How much he's really missing.

Ref:
(1) A Glesga grin: Glasgow, Scotland — slashed with a knife from ear to mouth/chin.
(2) would not
(3) White Lightning: A strong, easily available and very cheap cider/alcoholic brew.
(4) give
(5) do not
(6) dae away: put in hospital/intensive care.
(7) a lethal weapon when put to wrong use.
(8) please don't do that.

IT STARTED WITH A TREE

Find stimuli,
Get out and see
There's life in a beech,
Take note.
So—I talked to the tree
And the tree said to me
'Take me down and receive what I tell you.

Naturally there's wood in the trees, and bore in a hole,
And hardwood to carve bits and pieces
Molecular energies, minerals, give gravitation:
That leads then to carbon fixation.

The rings that we bear we carry with care
I'm a hundred years old don't you see?
Each ring is a lesson; each branch has its season.
Write down: and I'll carry you through
To friends growing up; looking down,
Far away,
In a creak tribute to Amazonia.

The going is good and we'll go with the flow
Of the time and tides,
And meet up when we're high in the Andes.

On Black Esk's fair bank a bird took the pip,
And there from the seed, root was given.
Quick on the uptake and fighting for joy,
I looked out up
And reached for the heaven.

I've grown sturdy in time and mature at the edge
Of the river you're standing beside,
Where animals roam and leaves offer shade
In a habit offensive to none.

The ants carry loads and burrows are there,
For the animals roaming the fields.
The bark's rough and ready—
Lenticular in nooks and crannies.

Goodwill is channeled fixated in growth,
Ascending as sap in the phloem and xylem,
Of trunks that are high as a mast.

And lumber when hollowed and sculpted with reason
Advances canoes for the Incas who paddle their own.
Cell mixing equals differentiation.

There's 'Goblings' on high—they're snug in the home
Of the nest that the cuckoo is robin'.
There are veins and there are threads
That join us for seasons untold,
Till we age, cleave and leave—
And join in recycling in old Mother Nature.

So let's leave behind our base nature
And travel on current and tide,
To branch out from beech to the sea.

From the lea of the Esk to the mouth of the Forth
The journey there hasn't been long.
Just a few hundred seasons and many good reasons
For traveling, traveling, on.

From North Sea to South, to bypassing Dover,
By Calais and then to the West,
We join with the current wending its way
O'er the ocean.
And meet with the winds
And the Atlantic waves
Of the beckoning over before us.

We'll travel from North to South, East to the West
And take in a lesson or two
Of swirling content meant to give us a hand
And wave us along the main highway.
If we don't listen well and do as they tell

We're going to end up cast out in Mongolia.
The fish of the sea and the ether above all lend us—
Their beauty is second to none.
And each bears the fame of that special name
Of the man who gives each one his claim.

I can see the nation taking shape,
By the light of the silvery moon.
The equatorial continent ledge
Is shaped like the mouth of the spoon.

Oh counter the current and pull us right in—
Gravitational leaning behind us.

All 2,700,000 square miles of deltaic deep deposition
Is second only to the Nile—
In length and breadth it's awesome.
So come with me said my talking tree
And on we'll go to meet them.

Midcourse through jungle, navigation is slow,
It's hampered by floods and by rapids.
Yet, moving along, we'll meet with the flora and fauna
In uplands,
And eventually see Marañon.

Ucayali unites to go with the flow,
Orinoco is joining us too.
They'll meet us as swell as we journey on
To end up in Central Peru.

Overwhelming the senses, snaking the continent,
Amazon takes us upstream
Cornell University has its own lab
To study the lush and the green.

Complex and smooth bark plates from the tree
And honey is luxury given.
The word of the harvest is shared by the family of man
In that tiny haven.

On we go up to meet with the folks
Who've called in to study the planet.
Hydrologists see, biologists be,
Entomologists beetle around.
Scientists study log rhythms,
Bio geochemists just nod and agree.

Ichthyology studies the fish of the season
Of the time it is bedded within.
Botanists gather and gaze at the wonder—
Creation is letting us in.

The Amazon branches at dizzying heights
And headwaters rapidly fall,
Ucayali goes left—cutting deep—as a canyon.
But we'll journey on via Nazareth town,
And stay on the road that is right.

Carved high in the Andes astonishing facts,
Gneiss and schist, slates and slants,
Snowbound peaks, ridges,
All harbor the sounds of the birds.

Songs live there—
Right on the range of the movement
That's second to none.
Near the flight and the might of the condor.

And up draughts and thermodynamics and drifts
Propel the air traffic above us
In pulls of fresh air and carbons and balance
Along the main highways of radiance, energy, wonder.

Bright snow-capped peaks rise above windswept plateaus;
And over the hill the Pacific—
Where the winds and the waters potentially blow
In rhythms of lifting, and laying, and shoaling.

But for this time we will not go there.

We've almost reached our journey's end;
Let me show you now, my friend,
The strength of the pathway we're taking.

My friend is the seed of the ground that we're in
And mature in the character given,
Is part of the grace full of joy and of beauty and giving.
Ingrained with strength and carried and given,
You'll meet us in church—in the pew.

The soil here is good and good here is grown
And much is the harvest that's riven
And down at the wayside tangled and torn
Are the briars and the bushes and bruises and burns
Of the roots that are gnarled and are snarled and are broken
That will choke us and trip us and use us and strangle,
And kill us—if that ground is given.

So straighten, my friend and take up my hand
And call on the name of Our Father
Then kneel down and pray and most surely know
That there's help, and we grow, in
Our Savior.'

AUTUMN

A time to be borne along, triggering change,
As days grow much dimmer and winter's in sight
The stage of maturity's time and its reason
Hints of the fall of the color; vibrant, best seen
In the intricate weaving threads' weathering scene.

With gentle restraining (the Hand from above)
Means drama's displayed as snap, crackle and scrunch;
Of wildlife preserving nutritional hoards
Of apples and nutkins, squashed pumpkins, and more.
Harvest's thanksgiving each year brings to life,
As the temperatures drop by the inch, and decrees
That the covering blanket moves south through the trees.

Crisp air of the mountains.
Take time—relax and enjoy.

Tread on the mufflers—kick, pile, scrunch
Leaves in the glory, not covered in green,
In the swift flowing current that moves down the stream,
The furnished and burnished prime colors of old—
Gold, and orange, and crimson, and bronze.
Lightens our sense of gifts from afar.

Harvests are waiting, all ready to store—
Full of dropping and lifting and laying and more,
Of the wholesome and pre-serving hoards.

And munchkins and leaf peeping poppers
Around hardwood leaves clutter and jam.
Gorge maple syrup sap demystifies
When morning—as peace—prospers life to new dawn.
Defrosting awakenings, still blurring the morn's
Conscious ovation, as mist—
Lifting peace over rural hill, valley, clad mountains, and town.

Chloroplast masks trapping nature's night chills.
Degrees cooling rapid variations of skill,
In the poet and writer the sage and the pen
Inspiring quite different variations in men.

Combine and harvester—fruits gather in,
Thanksgiving, moon.
Take time to be still.
Relax and take note.

Fruition has tingle and air has a bite;
The sign of the good vibrant colors hang out
Dropping softly—as blankets grow thicker,
And coats that are fur-lined grow heavy and warm.
Fires burning bright in each nook and cranny—
Show windows alight;
Smell smoke, leaving coal fires' magnificent scent.

The bright show and spectrum, the brilliance, the hue
Of the timing—is right for the spin of the cycle
That moves us along field works' highway—
'Neath the canopy sky of forget me not blue.

Heart, hearth, home, bring out the best
Round the meal at the table of nature's true store.
Bidding us welcome to join with them all
Where the peak of the nation is New England's shore,
And *Rock of the Ages* in churches is sung.

In white steeple dominion the plain truth is one
Of reflecting on teachings depriving no-one
Of the bounteous harvest.

All debris—keep clear.

CATALONIA
Barcelona.

Steeple bells chime 'midst spires holding dear
All that they've held to for 2000 years.
Eternally flaming, the fires burning bright
In the hearts of the dear folks, knowing who's right.

And wrought work Ionian iron is hewn,
Uncluttered, inspiring, the touch of man's kind.
Cathedral and masonry's spires intertwine
As scene from the rooftops: a Catalan view.

In the Rock of the Ages—the house used for prayer—
Age of the nation and beauty is bare
Of the clutters and gutters that tangle and snare.
The people so pleasant—abiding in Grace.

Brilliant plants, shining sky, sea and shore,
Carvings and chapels and palm leaves and more:
Dates, fig tree leaves, gardens, and troughs.
Wide view of the city spread angled beneath
The spire of Our Lady—Saint Maria del Mar.
Look down from the steeple for all there—to say
'Mediterranean waving, interweaving of Thee'.

VASHONII

'Steer clear', said the Admiral, 'steer mighty clear.
The angels above us are holding us dear.'

'Steer clear' says the frigate—the old order given.
Tradition is taking us—pathway's to Heaven.

'Don't go' says the bad one,
Chaffing, hard bitten.
'Don't go where
The Lord is And all is forgiven'.

'Don't go where He tells you,
The Cross and the way
Of the light, love and giving,
Don't go' says the free for all, 'naught there is living'.

'We'll go' say the sailors, 'we'll go and away
From the order of Satan, carrying and pitching'.
Set the keel, move the doldrums, leaving them yonder
To wither, decay and to panic and ponder.

Unsavory, wormwood and groveling low,
Seduced by the father of demons and kings
Who for each one so captured maliciously sings.

We'll pray that our Good Lord, the Highest of Heaven
Will bring to You glory, repenting, forgiving,
The ones of the snaring and tearing and driven
To spoil and to ruin what from You is given.

Hot air and ballooning—and huffing and puffing,
Won't oil paint the pathways of life worth the living.

We thank You Our Lord for all that is true
May they, in repentance, be brought home to You.

JERUSALEM

Nestling on ancient Judea's Biblical hills
Capital city, Jerusalem, state.

Confines of city in fortified walls.
Centre of conflicts—and wonders oft told
By the prophets, the priests and the kings,
Of the Jewish to whom
All the land has been given.
Not always perfect, not hidden from view,
Spirits conflicting and factions not new;
Let's not dwell in distractions opposing to You.

Multi-racial and settled—the rampart, the view
Of the olive greens, highways, sky blue color and hue.
Bring us closer to Heaven Lord, closer to You.

Overwhelming, Gethsemane: 'not My Will but Thine'.
Betrayed by Iscariot—and payment is given.

There at the center as they called 'Crucify'
Is Golgotha's hillside—and Calvary's Cross.
There is such suffering, and in cruelty and pain,
In the mocking hostility—the crown and the thorns
Are borne by our Savior—the King of the Jews.

To the people accusing, no basis—such loss.

And Mary Your Mother—her heart pierced with sorrow
Abiding, and watching, as Your Son, our Savior,
Grows weaker, much weaker—'Father forgive them',
Till Hell's deed is done,
And scripture fulfilled by the death of Your Son.

Joseph from Arimathea did come,
To lay our dear Savior in death's earthly tomb.

Mary Your Mother, Magdala, and more
Have witnessed the tomb with that open door.
The Savior has risen—to go on before
Testifying disciples, who see and believe.

The third day, Ascension, to Heaven You've gone
To return here with Glory, the world is to come
To the Savior, our Jesus—our thoughts praising high.
To the Father, the Spirit, we call 'Glorify'.

The Church there is Holy, the temple You teach
The way of that taking, the stations;
The cross there on Calvary,
Reminding us all of the pathway for nations
Where You gave Your all.

Let's not be complacent—that pathway is true
And all that may enter will find there, is You.

In that holy cathedral we meet there as one
Of the people, the nations, ecumenically bound
To accepting our Savior who died there for me,
That love freely given to save us for Thee.

The church has its schisms—it's not always right
Or led in the way Lord to keep You in sight.
We do well to remember, to keep You in view
And trust in the glory, the gospel, the giving,
Not earthly or dearthly by man so oft riven.

Scripture is Holy to keep us on track,
And lessons in opposite—throw them right back
To the devil who gives them—for none can compare
To the beauty the choosing, the ease and the care
You are taking to keep us in You.
Wholehearted commitment is joy Lord of You.

On old city rooftops every day worth the living,
Red tiles and washing lines, water tanks,
Warmed by the sunlight and sun fresh and clean,
Bright and airy.
And chimneys to sniff down—
To meals smelling scary.
Look down on the market, place color and hue
We pray of our Savior we'll meet there of You.

And each one bears witness to love in man's kind
Dear Savior remember our loved ones behind
In the ages, who've gone on before.

And may many of Isaac and Ishmael, Christian and new,
In synagogues and monasteries, in dome,
In the rock,
Lay foundations of deeper in Thee.
In the City of David, in Zion, cry 'Holy, our Lord',
Whilst wailing and waiting Lord,
Waiting for Thee.

JAFFA GATE STING

Where the bugs bite, and the itch is,
Where we're looking swell,
I'm simply remembering that Jaffa Gate place
And then I don't feel—so well.

Bugs are made by You, and made to
Stay in their proper place.
They encroach by stinging host,
So in correct order, them dispel.

Buy ammonia, get your own y'a,
Buy a bug pen—dab it on.
In the meantime, get it clean time,
Managers: 'listen—disinfect'.

If they listen to travelers' wisdom,
Clientele will pass along
To the nations with glad tidings,
Jaffa Gate is clean again.

And the kitchen, will they listen?
Rip it out and start again.
Elbow grease and elbow over;

A strong sledgehammer
Will take the pain—
Out of the 'b' hives crawling northwards,
And the gutters on the floor.

Kitchen fitter—pay the bill time,
A good day's work will see them through,
And when it's finished a traveler's mealtime
Will look like food—time will tell the tale.

Time to start time, time to end time,
Get it done lads, get it done.

BETHLEHEM
24 December 2002.

Towards midnight this Christmas,
Skies blue and red,
Sun's set slow blanket—
Brings stars crisp set in space.

Nativity's setting—2000 years gone
When weary and pregnant,
No room at the inn—for Mary,
And Joseph on that winter's eve:
In biting conditions—heralds warm of new dawn.

Your birth wasn't easy, so humble, so clean
'Midst the cattle a lowing;
Angels claiming new birth
To the shepherds close by.

The time for our Savior,
Our Jesus, had come—to be born there of Mary,
Our Jesus, Your Son.

Mary, and Joseph, so careful, so warm
In that winter shelter, that roof—Your first home.
And into the manger your parents did place
The Son of Almighty—newly borne
Beauty, grace.

Oh Child of the manger—forgive us our sin.
Pray be central in all hearts, Lord, welcome us in—
As pilgrims and weary, the joyful, the lost.

To the settings of righteous—with You as our Head
Of the Church that is able. And to You we turn
For all goodness and beauty Lord—
All that is right.

Ah, Child of the Manger, in praise rightly given
Understanding, uprising, we kneel Lord, 'fore You.

Let none be confused by the teaching, the giving,
The answers, the living.
Each turn of the Bible's page wording, page praise,
Of Holy stability's
Wonderful wage.

FROM JERUSALEM
And On To: Jordan

Shem, Ham and Japheth from Noah did come
Through the Ark: of the Covenant
All our own trees descend.
Forty days in that vessel, water covering the land—
Dovetails of peace find at each rainbow's end.

Ararat's mountain: Shem's Semitic peoples
You'll not smite again.

So to: Hashemite Kingdom—mountainous view
History is steeped in the good and the true
Buck the wild donkey, goats, sheep, and more
Groups of small children—happy their eyes
Speak of Irbid, Salt Sea and salting.
Passing Jaresh—keep our feet on their ground

Van that is dusty, battered and worn,
Driver who's steady, knowing the score.
Hands face lines are settled, with smile taking care.
A clear friend and helpful—of fine Bedouin lore.

Down from the mountain top reaching Amman
Arena's reception is peaceful and calm.
Christmas trees twinkling, wood carvings at door.
Sandwiches heaped high
Chicken and lettuce, olive fruit and more.

Relax—seats to be sat in, leather and old.
Reflections: of mirrors, marbling crystal and glass,
And traffic that's heading away from me
Fast.

A week in surroundings meeting nothing but care.
Scarves' red chequered fringes—keep dust
From their eyes.

Soldiers are busy—swot—fly's on the wall.
Listening is easy—they've heard it before—
Britain's mad evil, and all that is caused
By the route of the father, and all who are lost.

'Intervene' is the message, You my soul doth restore.
Abuse makes me walk from British Embassy door.
Lethargy not allowed for, too hot sunshine's unkind,
My feet are well:
Treading, the path really worn,
In righteousness drawing up to Palace gate.

(*FAX RECEIPTS and LETTERS re
explanations are at the end of this poem.)

Wending the winding way—gates gold close behind,
Shadowing and shaded—leafy green is so kind
To the flagging;
Defences and minibus takes to hill up on high—
To the Court Royal Protocol
Where tea now is served.

Tumbling welcome water—
Humble making, humble be.

'Believe when I tell you all is not well—
Sanctions are taking the pathway to hell.'
Out with the paper saying 'not a word'—
Onwards and outwards
To outwit' them all.

Ticketing—(billet to British Embassy's Crown)
Cool and efficient in that environ
Helpful, respectful, (the cat's a bit shy.)
But room there for moving and pausing to store.

Out by the gatehouse journey rightly won—
Awesome, exposing, respectful and fun.

His Royal Highness Abdullah—43rd direct line (*Sunni*)
From Mohammed the Prophet, distinction is set.
Revealing—that journey—far beyond the request
For help in the moment of Embassy's stress.

Out by the airport Royal Jordanians show
A plane—thing of beauty—recommended to all.
I write this from Shannon—from London we've come,
All thanks due to those who know Allah there…
One of life's highways heralding new
Experience, wonders and joy.

Book binding is hampered, publication is slow
Fruition being hindered by the *coarse* of the law
Of the British contingent,
Snagging and snickering and brackish and more.

Crisis is critical—Bush's burning alarms.
Smokescreens in White House—while
Pentagon dithers and swithers and sways.
Public: 'focus attention on their mighty ways.'

But You are our Father, and Your answer given
Is seldom adhered to in their mighty haven.
So Father, please give them the help that is earned by
The wise and the faithful, the experienced and learned.

So gather and nourish the ways of The Father
In private and prayerful, in wisdom and honour.
And Father, we thank You for all that is given
To teach and rebuke us in earth's tiny haven.

May all find the glory that in You is given,
To all those who seek You and find,
We're forgiven.

Epilogue

Didn't get to Mount Nebo—
Moses saw Promised Land—
From where Joshua to Jericho walls
Went down with a bang.

But history is proving and shaking and moving.
While on to The Temple great
Worth is accruing.

Fax Receipts and Letters being referenced:

*Until 26 December 2002 address is:
c/o Jaffa Gate Hostel
Jaffa Gate
Jerusalem
Israel
Email address: rosewhitel@yahoo.co.uk
19 December 2002

For the Swift and Urgent Personal Attention of:
Her Majesty Queen Elizabeth II
Buckingham Palace
London
Via:

Geoffrey Adams
Her Majesty's Consul General
British Consulate
Nashashibi Street 19
Jerusalem
Israel

Re: ROSEMARY E. WHITELAW – PASSPORT
NUMBER (deleted for the purposes of this publication).
Onward travel to Jordan.

Dear Geoffrey Adams,

Until 26 December 2002 I shall be based in Jerusalem and Bethlehem.

On 26 December, whilst dealing with a book manuscript, I am required to travel to Jordan. I need to be able to pay lodgings, along with travel and food expenses.

For that reason I require swift access to money which is mine and which is publicly known to be.

In public recognition of this we require at this time an update re that funding—the details of which are already long term known to Queen Elizabeth II.

In order that an official reply be obtained we formally request that this letter be faxed for the personal attention of H.M. Queen Elizabeth II re the next step to be taken.

She can have at this late stage no allowance for pleading ignorance or innocence.

This referral is deliberately dated Thursday 19 December 2002 so that time is given for Her Majesty's reply to be formalized by 25 December 2002.

Copies are retained for book publication in the global and growing public domain. I require and request that speedy reply.

In Christ, (Signed)
Rosemary E. Whitelaw (*author Eliza Earsman*).

Ref. Freemasonry versus my family—1987—and the direct involvement of the then Queen Mother Elizabeth nee Bowes-Lyon, Patron of UGLE Freemasonry, Britain, and her daughter Queen Elizabeth II — monarch reigning then and now.

Funding being referred to: large amounts Pounds Sterling misappropriated by Freemasons and which legally belongs to me, along with expenses and compensation required over a fifteen years period for gross and professional negligence and malicious and vindictive criminal involvements.

Details are legally and officially held.

Requirements: Official reply from H.M. Queen Elizabeth II re her official involvements and in that capacity the answer as to what she intends to be doing/have done about this.

Message Confirmations re this:

1.

Fax: 00 44 207 930 9625.
Buckingham Palace, London.

Urgent & For

Personal Attention of.

H.M. Queen Elizabeth II

via

Her Private Secretary

Copies retained +
Copy to Foreign Office for information.

MESSAGE CONFIRMATION		19-DEC-2002 10:32 THU

FAX NUMBER: +972 2 5414157
NAME : VISA DEPT JERUSALEM

NAME/NUMBER	:	90044207930962S
PAGE	:	003
START TIME	:	19-DEC-2002 10:32 THU
ELAPSED TIME	:	00'44"
MODE	:	G3 STD ECM
RESULTS	:	[O.K]

2.

MESSAGE CONFIRMATION

19-DEC-2002 11:07 THU

FAX NUMBER: 972 2 5312117
NAME   : DOAR HAKNESET

NAME/NUMBER	:	048304322
PAGE	:	004
START TIME	:	19-DEC-2002 11:06 THU
ELAPSED TIME	:	01'20"
MODE	:	G3 STD ECM
RESULTS	:	[O.K]

רשות הדואר   העתק קבלה   22740

□ POSTFAX   □ TELEFAX   □ TELEX

רשות הדואר
Israel Postal Authority

POST FAX
THE ISRAEL INTELPOST
SERVICE

22740

1. Originating Office Knesset P.Office
Tel. No. 02-6514249

4. Pages/ 3
6. RE [X]

9. SENDER (including postal code)
R. Whitelaw
c/o Jaffa Gate
Hostel.
Jerusalem.

8. ADDRESSEE (including postal code)
H.M. Queen Elizabeth
II
Buckingham Palace,
London   9625

LIFE IN THE ARENA

Eye eye little spy I C U there.
Hotel lobbies—
And there's no one at home.

End.

ISAM

That courteous family Muslim man,
As father, son and husband,
He works all day, and honest pay,
Goes round and round to feed them.

He tells me of his family seven—
All going to university.
I hope they see how proud he'll be
To see them settled. Wholesome.

He'll go to England soon, one day.
His wife is going with him.
He's brought to mind how many kinds
Of transport there await them.

There's underground and overhead
And buses, trams, and taxing.
I still admit I must prefer the train of peace,
And peace of quiet—and camels.

It's morning and it's half past two,
He's made piping tea
Of mint and sweet, to share and share
And tell me of his teaching.

It is of You,
There is doubt—no possible deception.
I'd like to know he sees the gift he is,
Being someone special.

MIDNIGHT AMMAN
Amman Jordan—December 2002.

(Scottish Ritual Freemasonry's 'scripted' and illegal war in
Iraq broke out in March 2003. See also the book
Days of Elijah: A True Story by
Eliza Earsman. ISBN 978-0-9556248-2-7)

Yawn. Yawn.
Embassy is broken down, Ambassador's* gone home,
*Christopher Norman Russell Prentice (born1954)
is the current HM Ambassador to Iraq (Baghdad),
the fourth appointed in four years.
British Ambassador to Jordan 2002-06.

Knotted Nita's (1) taking rest
And I am all alone—on Abdoun (2) streets
Talking, slowing down the pace,
And spinning out another night
Instead of taking place in cozy home
And heart-like snug, and life.

When all is said and done
Their Majesties (3) will pay;
The cost—of lifetimes held on ice,
And families being denied.

Not so pretty is it, the price there is to pay?
Tomorrow—thank our mighty Lord—
Remains another day.

Queen Liz II (4) grieves me,
Being subjected gives great sorrow;
At knowing just how much is lost
For families, circles, values.

I'm not really now respectful
To the one who knows no pain.
For those she's lost—
For those who've gone before her.

The lady (5) says 'I'm not amused'
And nor am I, I vouch for.
Too great the cost of all that's lust;
For greed, for hate, for evil.

I trust the lady's going to see
Accessories' costs too many,
While cardboard boxes shift as homes,
And shoe stores garner plenty.

The treasured troves are piling high
The empty barns o'erflowing.
Dear treasures in the heart, my love,
It's written in the annals.

Give ear: please listen, think, and then—offload.
Lighten stock piles massing heaps,
And sweep and swoop, and spring and clean
The chaffing, flooring, posing, fact:

Discern—receive—retrieve a grain
Of insight—honor—wisdom—reason.

(1) UK Vice Consul Amman in 2002
(2) district in Amman
(3) British Mountbatten-Windsor royal family
(4) Queen Elizabeth II Britain
(5) Queen Liz II—see above

BRITISH EMBASSY AMMAN
End of December 2002.

Jordanians. Wow.
So courteous—so calm.
Embassy tea:
'Have a cup, it's for free'.

We know what is missing in the link and the chain
Of the British controllers whose heads bang in vain.

McDonald's the café we're sitting within,
The night is much warmer, much cooler without
Nita the 'Grand One'—vice-consul is she,
Qualities broker questions—and not only she.

*Reference following verse: letter/fax receipts can
be viewed at FROM JERUSALEM—see previous.*

'After 6 January '03' is the answer she's giving,
'Replies come through
From the House of the Windsor—
Their one at the top.'

6 January. Eh. No, no, dearie me,
They've had it
Since December 19, 2002.

Their Majesty's Queen (1), she's the monarch o' realm
That's dwindling before them and time will oft tell
Of the momentous madness since her reign began,
Of the reasons they've given, and given, too much.
And of boxes of hardboard and card, by The Strand (2).

'No stamp', says the Nita, so we're out in the cold,
Hotel Manager's right when he says they're 'not bold.'

The guard is so good, they're training her still
To have the good manners requirements instill.

Maybe some lesson she'll learn there some day
Of how to be courteous and learn from the men
Who offer the tea, the good and the warm
And those teachings they have
That wish no one harm.

Andrew (3) is funding
From some pecu*liar* place,
Masonic in glory and trying to save face.
He's surely not only in yon yonder dell.

Strangely, obviously, defiantly and very arrogantly,
They listen to the Devil who teaches so…
Well how much does he need for that Windsor tree?
'Very much of others',
But that's twixt
Thee and me.

The police at the gate guard so fresh and so clean.
I know of the privilege to have been close within
The confines of circles; and their answer's given.

'No problem and we'll help. Just give us a ring.'
The number is written and signed by their hand.

Still no sign of Nita, working as paid to.

Deviant the system that beckons them in
And causes commitment to sign after sin.

Not some faceless mystery, history will tell
Of the deeds of the Nita, and career moves?
Ah. Well.

Not as well as she's hoped—for the details contained,
In curriculum vitae are open to all.
No foreign official, untainted, unseen.
No attaché mysterious—detached from the wise
Is Nita the Humphrey, vice-consul
Grim Britain.

(1) Queen Elizabeth II of Britain.

(2) A dirty main street in inner city London where homeless people bed down/on cardboard at night.

(3) Andrew Mountbatten-Windsor — son of QE II above.

HEAVENS ABOVE

Astronomically speaking, light years away:
Masses, moons, planets, clusters,
Point us Lord heavenwards
Accelerating earth's bright new busy day.

Astro encompass, astonish, astound;
Part of attraction's mean distance, not sound.
Decorum enhancing—no clamour up there,
Out there in space time, wonder and stare.

Telescopic intervention,
Hubble's huddle huddle, nuts and bolts
Refracting nebulosity,
Piercing time and narrow space.

Hands of Our Father, Providence, Grace,
Illumine in evidence earth's tiny face.
Balance in harmony, composition in view,
Solar altitude, energy, planets anew.

Night-light when falling near the end of a day
Impacts in the gilding, the ochre and gold,
Catching sign of the ancient, sidereal time—
Dynamic novations* since before we were born.

Three Wise Men journeyed by that Heavenly light
Directionally yearning, navigation in view—
Moving, not backward, bearing us on
Onwards to see Thee in earth's tiny form.

*****

Evolution is moving on, sign of the times,
Occurs to all species fighting strong to keep warm.
Collide in collusion amplifies waste,
Revolutions: 'world leaders—do well to know place.'

* *Nova ovations.*

ODE TO THE ODOROUS

("Jardines always was and still is a Scottish house
that kept The Sabbath—and everything else they
could lay their God-forsaking hands on.

No less than 32 senior partners of the
Jardine-Matheson Company have been drawn
from, and have their homes in, the author's home
area of south/south west of Scotland.")

***

Phew.

Applegirth records (1) Jardine ancestral tree.
In seed bearing branches is fruit turning sour.
The harvest is falling and rotting away
From the good—
Life disintegrating, degrading to all,
Compacting, composting, that wood us would bind.

They're seen of the father they follow behind
It's the one who is stalking their face, flesh, and s/kin.
Opium and jaded, Chinese and war (2),
Locked into leaching—
Each J.M. (3) I.D—
History's hideous egos lusting for more.

Strangling and sapping the goodwill of all,
Fruit of their harvests are bodies and souls.

Abominable conditioning;
Their reason,
The treason—
Monopolise greed.

Trapped in the tap root they glean to pass on,
Fruit of their season
Is taste and be damned.

Chieftain's degrees (4) smart Alec's his name. (5)
His good wife is Mary (6). Don't be misled.
They are thieving and plundering,
Rape, racket and ruin.

I thought I'd keep going,
But their nobble's no good.
Reaction?
My stomach won't take them.

No more.

In their return to the earth lies echos and grave,
To ash urn and silting, returned unto dust.
But cutting the cords, let us truss:
And—break free.

References:
(1) JARDINE OF Applegirth, Lockerbie—ancestral trees.
(2) Opium Wars of China—with the loss of many lives.
(3) Jardine-Matheson Company. See—history.
(4) Masonic Degree/s—Scottish Ritual Masonic degrees.
(5) Sir Alexander Maule Jardine of Applegirth, Lockerbie, Scotland. Died 2008.
(6) Lady Mary Beatrice Jardine—widow/of smart Alec.

See also: Days of Elijah: A True Story by Eliza Earsman.

THE FAMILY TREE

From: Days of Elijah: A True Story.
ISBN 978-0-9556248-2-7

Hardy and neat
I look a treat.
The housewife thinks so too.
They think I'm green,
They've seldom seen
The trials I've been through.

Green.
Green.
They bray.
I'll have my say.
Stop.
Look.
And listen now.

Small seeds of love (self)
The family tree (five generations maternal.
three generations paternal)
For generations grew. (time span 100 years
—same time and same place)

In Truth and Light (openly and honestly)
It watered well, (well taught)
The watching Pruner knew. (Jesus. John 15:1-4.)

Small seeds grow strong
And straight and true
When they are nurtured well.
Mine grew until
The time was ripe (40 years)
To blossom, and then …
Well.

The bees begin to gather
They swarm,
And was in their sting.
The vultures wait
To pick the flesh
Of all that might have been.

Fool's gold they saw.
Their thoughts revolved around financial picking.
We'll use this tree and then we'll see
A windfall for the taking.

They chose their time—and Satan knew
(For he had stalked his prey)
A 'lite' they had—and well he knew
He'd have his evil way.

The time was right
To blossom forth
Good seed was to mature.
They pulled me down,
They tried to kill.
They hurt me to the core.

Cold storage treatment
Meant to fool the masses didn't work.
Cold storage meant plans put on ice
But warmth will do the trick.

THE CIRCUS COMES TO TOWN 1987

(The Moffat and Dumfries areas of Scotland
at that time.
From: Days of Elijah: A True Story.
ISBN 978-0-9556248-2-7)

Sickening Sophia (1) saw a chance
To work on power for glory
A Nobel Peace Prize took her eye
And so she said "we'll have that". Aye,
But time will tell the story.

Mary, Mary, (2) quite contrary
Was pulled in to the fore
The spirits moved at their command,
God knows just what's in store.

Odette (3) was there to call the tune
To dance at her command
On Hallowes ground—just don't ask why,
We've planned it so you'll do or die.

I didn't know a thing of this
I saw it differently.
An understanding of the time Meant I was free to choose.

God's path in truth and light and love
Was right without a doubt;
They didn't want, they didn't see
What truth was all about.

Their malice was beyond belief,
They loused it up, no doubt.
But time will tell the tale of this
And what it's all about.

Roll up, roll up, we'll draw the crowds.
We'll push and pull and sway.
The spotlight's fixed, it's focused on
This one (4) who got away.

Right on cue they all arrived.
The clown in frills and flounces (5)
Good Heaven's up above, dear sir,
Repentance He announces.

The puppet mistress (6) pulls the strings
To dance, she'll call the tune.
The strings attached held no appeal…
We'll drop her fairly soon.

The whip is cracked, the show is on.
The glitter blinded some (7).
I trust they'll learn to discern
Right from all that's wrong.

High social circles round about
Hid con-folk slyly mocking.
The ways and means of some like these
To honest folks is shocking.

Church men (9) when approached re this
Make fun of all that's happening.
They are so wrong to want condoned
Baal and its way of working.

The path God calls—the one I choose
Is right I know for certain.
Does not equate, I most surely state
With church manipulation.

Dark and devious was the plan
To cause confusion in the land.
Side by side they worked in pairs
But now—their turn to face the glare.

"We'll pass it off as right" said they.
"We'll make a killing, ho."
But truth to tell and tell it well,
They'll reap what they do sow.

One worm will turn the barrel bad
If it's allowed to stay.
Oh boy, oh boy, am I so glad
That God has had His say

And so the nation pays the price
For evil manifest
By fools who play with fire
But then: they never have confessed.

Grey Britain has rejected much.
The Hand of God it's shunned.
May You have mercy on the souls
Of those who've so much ruined.

There is no going back in life.
One can stagnate and wither.
But all of those who have the choice
Can try to work together,

For all that's right before Dear God
And firmly centred there
We can progress through Christ Our Lord
And live, and work, through prayer.

Appendix:
(1) Amelia Sophia Weatherall nee Keswick—ex Deputy Lord Lieutenant for Dumfries and of the Jardine-Matheson Company.
(2) Lady Mary Soames (daughter of Sir Winston Churchill).
(3) Odette Marie Celine Hallowes (formerly married to Peter Churchill). Formerly of: Rosedale, Eriswell Road, Walton-on-Thames, England.

The above three are interlinked by marriage.

(4) Self.
(5) Right Rev. Professor Robert Craig, Moderator, in 1987, of the Church of Scotland.
(6) Odette Marie Celine Hallowes.
(7) Church of Scotland clergy.
(8) Several belonging to the Conservative Party e.g. the now deceased Sir Hector Seymour Peter Monro of Williamswood, near Lockerbie
(9) For example The Right Reverend George Leonard Carey, Archbishop of Canterbury, and Reverend Doctor Geoffrey Edward Winsor Scobie, 3 Norfolk Crescent, Bishopbriggs, Glasgow, of the Scottish Episcopalian Church and of staff/ Glasgow University. Scobie is one the most awful people I have the misfortune to meet.

If these people persist in causing problems more of the names are going to go public. For example:

(10) John MacInnes Boyd, ex-Her Majesty's Chief Inspector of Constabulary, Scotland. Chief Constable of Dumfries and Galloway Constabulary, Dumfries, in 1987.Address: Beechwood, Lochwinnoch Road, Kilmacolm, Renfrew, Scotland.

(11) The Solicitor General for Scotland for the year 1987 — Peter Lovat Fraser, Baron Fraser of Carmyllie. Address: Slade House, Carmyllie, Arbroath, Scotland. DD11 2RE

(12) Jardines of Applegirth, Lockerbie. Named members of the family who resided in the area during 1987:

Sir Alexander Maule Jardine, born 1947 died 2008.

Succeeded his father in 1986 as Chief of the Clan Jardine, and his wife:

Lady Mary Beatrice Jardine: ex of Little Dyke, Dalton, Lockerbie, now of Ash House, Thwaites, Cumbria LA18 5HY.

(6) John Orr, Sir. Chief Constable, Dumfries and Galloway Police, 1990-1994. Assistant Inspector of Constabulary for Scotland 1994-95. Retired Chief Constable—Strathclyde Police.

GLASGOW
Cell Block's Hell.

He was dragged up, drawn in,
Slashed and beaten; broken.
He was backed up, knocked down
And banged against the wall.

Survival skills were teaching him and well;
Softened by the blows he was forced to look
And look—and look again.

He knew who he was.
Long hours had been spent in the learning.

He was okay. I know him.
I can vouchsafe there's a man—
And a half in there I like to know.
He's doing well.

The 'system' was unkind.
The 'Riddrie*' has long been known as
Barbaric, malicious and unjust
And much more besides, but—
Let's just say 'unkind'.

He's done his time.
He's not even sure there was a crime.
Caught up with others
Not even sure are they.

Would there have to be one?
I'm not saying there would.
Maybe his face was a ready fit for a polis' boot.

'Look *b…right'* says he, 'keep yer head above them
An' dinnae let them see. It's me that's sane—
No' them or they.

Joe has speed.
He's fitba' daft—he has talent in the making.
He's decent, thoughtful, decent, kind.
'Here's a coke' says he as he slaps it down,
'And one for me.
I share it 'cos I'm meant to'.

He's trained—to zoom along a hotplate
In thirty seconds
Flat tray in hand, and at the ready.
Off at the flick of a switch.

'Veg. Veg.' says he 'can ye no' cook them right?
Can't ye see they're no' still growing (mould).'

He's doing haircuts now.
He's trading well.
Razor sharp is Joe—and a No. 1 is all he knows.
Fair dinkum—
For anyone wanting to look like a Barlinnie prisoner
For only—'£3 ahead'.

He's done his stint, now he's seldom skint
In his wee barbershop emporium.

He's hyperactive.
Not surprising for a teenager confined by rule
To one square wall of space
With no outlet for energising power.
No allowance there for a healthy outpouring
In a hard day's graft.

Over the wall when or if he gets the chance
An odd ball—and no messing.
He's keen to please:
No problem—to those who care.

He's not the one causing problems—
Other people are.
Mop and bucket spilling blood—
He's seen it all before.
He'll mop it up behind the ones
They're knocking to the floor.

They're letting him go—tomorrow.
Seems he's reached their limit.
The warders said they'd break him.
Joe boy said he'd make them.

Tomorrow he's going to be dumped—
Back in the *mean mean* city**
With a paper bag and the words
'Her Majesty's Prison'
Or—as is so often correctly defined—
'At Her Majesty's Pleasure'.

I wonder if she knows
Just how much her pleasure is costing?

Without food or clothes or money or shelter—
Or any means of finding any
He is expected to thrive.
Friends of the earth—where are we?

He's lost. Yes.
Five years of teenage growth
And his mother's tender loving.

They never even knew him.
They banged him up—
They didn't get to screw him.

He's kept his head above them all—
And though his knees are shaking
At the thought of moving forward,
He can't look back.
There's nowhere there he hasn't been.

Just for this day he is in limbo
And in understandable fear—
The day after the morning before,
And the day before the morning to come.

Though tough it's been and hell, he'll win.

* *Riddrie—Glasgow's Barlinnie Prison/Jail.*
** *Glasgow.*

CHUNK

Said to me the old fossil embedded in time
'Go to the mountaintop; look down,
Espy terrain that is awesome. Survey the scene
Of valleys that stumble, so vivid, so green.

Small in significant atop rocks we stand
With hands shielding eyes longing view of the land.
Peaks and troughs, crags, nooks, crannies,
Shimmering dust,
Chips from the old blocks in deep waters thrust.

River rough at the edges tumbles along,
Boulders plug, fishes fly,
Skiffing low roots, rocks and trees,
Sluggish, sluicing, round the bend.

Upriver, downstream, flow limits sink and swim.
Deepening waters 'tribute currents drift
Shifting rocky bottoms shallows bar.
Survival's fast food maze foray.

And on that clear day—that very warm day
Nodding breeze day, and pastures new,
Strong strokes end of twilight, hanging stars,
Moon, and velvet sky day—
That river ran to and met
The sea.

SCENE FROM THE BACKGROUND

Lighthouse—out skerries—beckons safe journey by
Rock chips and chunks formed many million years ago.
Lifeboat and good folks—
Going down to the sea.

1000's of naughty* miles;
Tiny bird's—span in the hand.
Chirrups and delicate—
Not storing in barns.

Gentle and warm air hitting the land,
Scrapes daisies' spinning deli-coats**,
Tiny buoy and bobbing gulls.
Waters, still, glacial, mirror each breeze.

Lamp-posts on either side frame in the view,
Strugglings in of amber light—
From flicker, gleam, to glow.

To the left sails at sunset a competent crew.
Sleepy lilies in the field show forget me not hue.
Seals curve and carve to play,
Fish reap and sow.
Child's voice skooters in/away;
Away to bed they'll go.

Smugglings—in silence—beauty's gifts from the sea.

* *Naughty—nautical (miles)*
** *Deli-coats—delicate coats.*

OLLIE

Ollie was a little cat—his eyes with beauty glowing,
And everywhere that Ollie went
His tale was in there, showing.

Underneath a car they put our Ollie. He did wonder
Just what he'd done to know the fate—
Being kicked out, put asunder.

Along came Dee and she did say
'This isn't right; I'll listen.
To this cruel fate I mustn't let poor Ollie go.'
No wonder.

So in came Dee and spoke with Mogs.
'Bring Ollie in' says she.
So Mogs did listen carefully,
And Ollie came as brother.

Oh Olls and Mogs we love you two,
And Johnny does so also.
He took his part and cared for both
When Dee to Oz did wander.

Ollie does contentment show,
No badness in him; beauty.
He showed his love of heart and home,
His family, care, attention.

In garden Olls did sleep around
'Midst plants secure and flowers.
From bench he did come in for tea,
Whenever he was called to.

He liked his Gran when she did call
He took her just for granted.
And she does note: appreciation of his need,
His self-respect, acceptance.

Now Ollie's gone to that safe place
Where little cats are called to,
And asking Dee and Johnny —
'Live long, live well, and please go on.'

To Dee and Johnny — 'love you.'

CANUTE

Water's edge: Canute
King
'Turning the tide?'

'Cannot'
Says King 'Nute
K'not (for miles).

'Can you not
King 'Nute?
Surely you can.'

'No, no, no' says Canute
'No, no, not a one.'

HARBOR

Fog curtains the fiords—
Lochs, laughing lanterns, fishing boats,
Harboring fleet glimpses—
Dawn fringing the view.

Mist now is lifting.
Sky larking lazy gulls
Seeing and sawing,
Swooping and swishing,
Stomping, chipping web feet
Tuning and squawking,
Splatter and cry.

Sssh.
Hearken—a tiny bird's song.
Tiny hands, weight and feat.

Sky's summer shimmer
Shelters blue setting sail.
Boats float, baubles toss, rust's set in bolt.
Juggle tackle '*chuckle chuckle* —weathering and tethering,
Knowing dinghy old ropes,

Clouds lessen, and clear blue sky,
Cast off the old clothes,
Sun's beat on distant hills,
Pipes, dreams and distance, calm.
Crowd cover nil.

Rock stratas, clamber down.
Sea-tide's shrinking the beach
Going down—plank, plink, plant.
Still—crowd cover's nil.

Cockleshells and heroes—convoys, old scene.
Remember: soldier/sailor boys,
War worn and grim?

No??

Shallow the water line—waves rushing in
I'll weigh up the options of staying put and still,
In these mountains and valleys,
'Midst the seashells and shale.

(Drop by and anchor here? Nope. Not a chance.)

Move on with our Dear Lord, away to pastures new,
Pacific Northwest islanders,
Puget sounds and pleasant green.
Orca whales be calling us
From the U.S.—calling on.

Back in the present
Fast forwarding, reel.
Steering—not stealing—
Now that battle's won.

Account is for clearing—and H.E.R.* must learn
Decent folk are helpful—respect must be earned
For the way that is truthful.
'Cause shallow the fault-line—
And the abyss lies deep.

No getting away from the fact that we're borne
As babies—not baddies—as sometimes is learned.
Discernment is easy, Gospel pages turn true.
Mull over a new leaf—think over and learn,
The right Day of Judgment—and accounts for us all.

*H.E.R. = Highness Elizabeth Regina (HM Queen Elizabeth II of Britain).

STORM

A ship lay safe and laden in a harbour
The cargo sane and safely settled in,
The storm approaching hadn't yet been tethered
'Judge Dread' was making headway to the scene.

'Too late. Too late.' onlookers cry:
The ship's already sailed.

Deep in their bones, and in the shadows
Sound sailors, hands out, stand and stare and bear and grim.
The growling old storm pocket is
Known as being smart.

An old fire blazes—the chamber awaits.
'Stone cold and dead we're going to be,
If this old ship goes down.'

Depths charge and underworlds dwarf,
Intruders swing and leap and bite.
They scratch and skewer,
Grasp and sting and steer,
Shifting sand and balance, rudder
Batten hatches. Shake and fear.

Graze and gallop, growl and wallop,
Grab, engulf, grind and chew.
Shiver, splinters shrivelling timbers,
'Wreak and havoc, 'ere we go.'

Old storm continued raging
Whipped and battered coast and shells,
A serious undertaking, and then:
Storm ran out of fuel.

'King Cool' changed gear.
He stopped and looked and listened—
He let the skylight in.
Pristine silver wedges opened,
Sun hammered waves to simmer down.

Quietly amid the story,
Growth which storm clouds just can't dim.
Tranquil face and precious wonder,
Cracking smiles start channelling in.

A drizzled choir of seabirds
Outflank the tenor serenade,
Sea eagles dare to swoop and soar
Where neither ship nor courage ran aground.

Power's struggle reached a limit—
Accentuating prayer.

Prayer
Had
Been
Heard.

LEST SHE FORGETS.
Lest we.

Ref: Scottish Ritual Freemasonry, HQ 96 George Street
Edinburgh, Scotland. Britain's UGLE
Mountbatten-Windsor royal family
(United Grand Lodge of England) + second generation
Nazi 'Bones folk' (Skull and Bones Masonic Lodge USA).
House of Battenberg (anglicized to Mountbatten),
Am Hof, Wien, Austria. Obere.

Sun slid behind the mountains,
Missing links are entertained.
Decent dignity suspended—
Handloom weavers quickly thread.

Seas of blood and time and lives—
Shuttles cease, disintegrate.
Jack boots worn in closets,
Phony Phoenix* showing face.

Ref: *Phoenix bird emblem worn on Nazi regalia.
The Phoenix is rising from the ashes—of the WW2 (leading to World
War Three) Holocaust.

Clock shows five to midnight,
Death rings, the glass inverts.
Moles in holes push dirt and distance,
Britain's black, hands dripping blood.

Duke of Kent (1) and 'Mad Mick' Michael (2)
Skull and bones, and aprons torch—
There's a conflagration burning,
Plumes and trees and families spent.
Ref: (1) Duke of Kent, Britain's No. 1 Freemason/ UGLE.
(2) Prince Michael of Kent/his place in Freemasonry's intended
'New World Order'.

Smokescreens clear.
Detect: Mountbatten-Windsor royals.
Royal family—end of line.
At the crossroads of contention,
Jezebel* sups from venom vine.
Ref: *Elizabeth nee Bowes-Lyon, mother of Queen Elizabeth II of
Britain. Died 2002.

'Mid their darkened spirit tentacles,
Brain cells are thin upon the ground.
Evil Scottish Ritual's allies
Reach and breach the Governor's Crown*

Ref: *Queen Elizabeth II, reigning monarch of
Britain, Governor of Church of England — HQ is at Canterbury, Kent.

Malice, oppression, destruction, deadwoods,
Madame's whipping lash and sin.
Brain power's sparse and headgear spaced-out,
From British history, scenes are grim:

Shipped, starved, burned, killed,
Maimed and evil torture, slaughter.

The dirt track leads to old BP*
Bustards circle, vultures fly.
The golded gildfish cages
The cuckoos robbing ring.
Ref: *Buckingham Palace, London

Global goslings look for mothers,
Mothers take their place, removed.
Parents — clothed in righteous anger —
Will take the H.E.R* (the bat) apart.
*Highness Elizabeth Regina — British monarch.

Their old flag 'Folly' slips and wavers.

Canterbury wolves are checking lyings,
Those which grow and glow will bounce.
Equerries bow — they scrape, and finger points —
Dehumanizing cell-group Cullen* stinks.

*Ref: *Cullen House, Cullen, NE Scotland. An Ogilvie/Kent holding.
North of Balmoral Castle.*

No room for sane at H.E.R old inn —
Chief priests and cult of Baal consort.
Blast thunder, canons mammon worship —
Turn the tables on their rot.

Satan resents. In the frame — the peasants revolt.

Rothschild's occult Zion —
And why the rebel cause?
Remember Adolf Hitler, World War Two,
And all that cost?

Adolf* was a Rothschild boy,
Wrath's house, Am Hof,
Vienna's Jesuits. Obere.

*Ref: *See family trees of Mayer Amschel Rothschild/Salomon Mayer
Rothschild.*

Stoke, shovel, smoke, billow, hovel, fuel covens*.
Cullen's Bismarck and H.E.R U-boats prowl.
Earnest warning, signals there.

*Ref: *Scottish Ritual Freemasonry's lodges/meeting places of Satan.*

Chests haul—lug baubles, bangles, coffins,
Jangle, bodies, limbs and souls.
Rats run—the sly folk mocking, con and laugh.
Their tryst with evil—knowing.

Lil' old Lizzie Windsor (1), twisted—
SAD (2) and smug—foreboding rain.
They nod and hood and wink and smash
Humbling storms are due, as gain.
Ref: (1) Elizabeth Mountbatten-Windsor—monarch.
(2) SAD Seasonally Affected Disordered/Eschatology/end age.

Scaffold nooses tighten grip,
Colliding facets hang with ease.
Mugs duped, lassoed and swinging,
'Et tu brutes' Death says—in sway.

In their 'theater' of World War Three—
Remember World Wars One and Two—
Armored cars, and tanks, nuclear and guns:
'Final solution' pounding.
Nazis liquidations—pending.

Windsor Castle, full moon—
Witch's broom and rising hoar.
Enslaved in vain, the gropers'
Smelly crown-fish boxes sore.

Central to the cooking pot is Lil (1)—
And she doth know.
Bitches gurgle, cauldron bubbles.
Scalding out are skull and bones.
Hoodwinked Keswicks (2) carry, scurry, spin and lie
And web deceit.
Ref: (1) H.E.R.—monarch Britain.
(2) Keswick family of the Jardine of Applegirth/Jardine-Matheson
Company. Component inner circles of the British royal family.

Bush (1) as bad and beady, UGLE,
Strut's Hitlerian war. Salutes.
Batons pass in White House—
War HQ—compacted zeal.
Bad-eye Brown (2), mad-eyed Blair (3)
And the Rothschilds (4), masquerade.
Ref: (1) George W. Bush and his father before him.
(2) James Gordon Brown—SR's British Prime Minister ex Chancellor
of the Exchequer.
(3) Anthony Charles Lynton Blair—now Scottish Ritual's
'Middle East envoy'.
(4) Rothschild dynasty/named members.

Fire consumes.
Tzar Nicholas II Romanov*—
Russia's court of *'take the Mick'* (1)
Robbin' Lehman (2) Robin Lenman (3) marks.
Rathaus orders new world in.

Ref: *Did he die in Yekaterinburg in 1918? Surfacing evidence
suggests not.
(1) Prince Michael of Kent—access details of the soon to be 'new'
Russian court.
(2) Lehman Brothers (LB Holdings Inc.)
(3) Robin Lenman, recently retired History Lecturer, Warwick
University, England—
access details of his first wife.

Their spiritual deviations
Are now being recognised
Their dammed abomination.
Tell old Satan—'go to hell.'

Remember there at Kishon,
On Mount Carmel—there and then.
Small as a man's hand—water,
Transpiration, cloud and rain.
(Ref: 1 King: 18)

Ponder—weigh—not lightly.
Entertaining? No.
Carry weight to scales on sane ground.
Scottish Ritual evil is hate.

Lord—have mercy on them
To the depths of their very souls
And save us Lord from a death like H.E.R's —
In the place of the fiery coal.

They do these things because
They know not Lord of Thee
Nor Mary Holy Mother, Queen,
Our joy, in destiny.

Deliver us from evil, Lord,
Our great Redeemer, King.
The kingdom, power and glory,
Lord—forever Thine.

Amen.

*****

www.ingramcontent.com/pod-product-compliance
Lightning Source LLC
Chambersburg PA
CBHW060951040426
42445CB00011B/1099